When Friends Ask About Adoption

Question & Answer Guide for Non-Adoptive
Parents and Other Caring Adults

Linda Bothun

Swan Publications

Library of Congress Catalog Card Number: 87-92207
ISBN 0-9619559-0-2

Swan Publications
P. O. Box 15293
Chevy Chase, Maryland 20815
U.S.A.
(202) 244-9092

For Ana and Jonathan

with special thanks to Erving and Lela and Vi, not to mention Dave, who finally convinced me to learn to use the computer.

Contents

Chapter One ~

"I've just scared my child."

Chapter One ~ "I've just scared my child," a mother from my children's school confided. "I was telling him that you had adopted your daughter. Now he's crying, afraid that you might give her back some day. I must not have said the right things."

I was concerned. Very concerned. That her child had experienced such fear about a friend. For my own children, one adopted, one a birth child, for whom that conversation might have harmful consequences. I knew instinctively that the attitude of her friends toward something as basic as her birth would affect the way she feels about herself.

Everything had been going so well for our family. Our children, at six and seven, understood at some level both the process of being adopted into a family and that of being born into a family. They had shown interest, acceptance, and some curiosity. But no fear. And now I wanted to find a way to lessen the possible impact, to remove the unnecessary fearfulness for the children, for hers and for mine.

I had experienced discomfort concerning adoption before, the discomfort felt by everyone involved, adoptive and non-adoptive parents alike, when the subject of adoption was brought up in the presence of our children and handled awkwardly. Until now, we adoptive parents have simply held our collective breath, hoping that people's responses would be kind and thoughtful. We grimaced when our beloved aunt introduced our family, making special note of the fact that "this is their adopted daughter and this is their 'own' son." But we found it difficult to correct her.

Parents of adopted children spend countless hours preparing themselves for the many circumstances related to adoption that they are likely to encounter. They read books, attend workshops and meetings, take courses, and help each other prepare for the questions that will eventually be asked of them by their adopted sons and daughters. Long in advance of the questions that usually appear at the various developmental stages—the five- and six-year-old questions, the nine- and ten-year-old questions, the adolescent questions, the adult questions—parents of adopted children have prepared themselves with concept bases, preferred phrases, and methods of presentation which will help the child to be comfortable with his adoption. They address questions such as:

> "What term shall we use to refer to the woman who gave birth to our adopted child?"

"How do I respond when my daughter yells in anger, 'But you're not my real mother'?"

The questions, most of them, are anticipated because of the research and sharing adoptive parents have already gone through. The couple has agreed upon responses they feel are constructive and helpful to the adopted child.

But what of the friends and relatives, teachers, club and activity leaders, other people significant in the lives of our adopted children. They will inevitably be involved as well. They will be the recipients of comments and questions, both from their own children who are playmates of our adopted children, and from our children directly. Which words should they use as they respond?

We adoptive parents have talked with these people about our excitement over adoption, about how fortunate we were to receive the incredible gift of a son or a daughter. But rarely have we shared with non-adoptive parents the circumstances we face which are unique to an adoptive situation:

~ attempting to be honest with our children and yet not burden them with more information than they are able to cope with at a given time;

~ reading no more into a question than is actually there;

~ dealing with our adopted child's emotions about his adoption, emotions which usually appear at various phases of his understanding;

~ deciding what information should be shared with siblings and friends and what is strictly private, for the adopted child only.

Adoptive parents literally spend years considering the subject of adoption. After that agonizing moment when they realized they couldn't or wouldn't bear a child, and they decided to have a family through adoption, the subject was foremost in their thoughts and conversations. Due to the scarcity of babies who need placement through adoption, a long wait nearly always ensued, punctuated by endless forms to complete, medical reports to submit, and accompanied by the ever-constant fear of being unacceptable to an agency.

But even after the countless hours the couple has spent preparing for adoption, and the baby is finally in their arms, they are faced with another realization—they don't know how or when to tell their child of his adoption.

How much more difficult, then, for the non-adoptive

parent to know how to present this delicate subject to his own child when asked.

This guide fills that void. It makes available to non-adoptive parents and other interested adults a synopsis of the most common concerns, questions, and mis-understandings about adoption. The guide is pur-posely concise and of manageable length. It does not attempt to exhaust any subject, but attempts rather to state the usual questions and give rather widely ac-ceptable answers.

The guide will prepare people for the eventual questions that will be asked of them by children. *It is not designed to be read to children or even to be discussed with a child until the appropriate question is asked.* It is rather a vehicle with which adoptive parents can gently edu-cate people who love them and who would be careful to say the right things if they only knew.

The guide is written with parents of young children in mind since generally it is the five- to seven-year-old who will begin telling his friends that he is adopted. Answers are therefore written for the most part to be useful for the younger child. Care has been taken to answer the questions fully but not to give more infor-mation than is called for at the time. If the child continues the questioning, he should of course be answered. Often, however, he will need time to consider an answer just as does the adopted child himself, and he will broach the subject with follow-up questions at a later date. The classic story is of the little adopted boy and his mother who were driving along in the car when the boy asked, "Mommy, did I grow in your tummy?"

His mother answered no and waited for the next question. It was, "Mommy, do you see the helicopter?"

It is suggested that non-adoptive parents also use care in answering the question that is asked but avoid forcing the issue. It is a common response to want to "tell the whole story," but too much information at once about this sensitive subject can produce fear in a young child.

Teaching about adoption is not something that is done once, completely, or forever. It is an on-going process. As long as a child, adopted or biological, feels he can talk openly about the subject with his parents or his peers, he will bring it up time and again and will ask whatever he is able to deal with at that time.

Adoption is so common in the United States that there is scarcely a person who doesn't know adopted persons or adoptive parents. A well-known syndicated advice columnist recently devoted an entire column to a letter from an irate adoptive mother, the mother of birth children and adopted international children, who was disgruntled and dismayed by the constant inappropriate attention and words showered upon her family by strangers and relatives alike.

Guidelines are needed, then, that will aid us all to attain caring attitudes and use caring words regarding adoption.

Chapter Two ~

Using and Sharing This Guide

Chapter Two ~ Questions in this guide are written as if they are being asked by a non-adoptive parent or by his child. Answers are written from the point of view of the adoptive parent.

Preferred answers will, of course, vary from family to family. In order to be useful to the largest number of people, the question and answer chapter provides:

Space after each answer so that notes or language of choice can be inserted; and

In some cases, multiple answers, all of which are found desirable by many adoptive parents. None is either right or wrong; it is simply a matter of preference.

Since the guide is designed to accommodate these differences, it can be personalized before it is shared. (See following example.) Adoptive parents can annotate the book to indicate the phrases with which they are comfortable as well as to include any personal comments or approaches they found to be successful.

EXAMPLE OF PERSONALIZED ANSWER

Q: What do you call the man and woman who gave birth to your adopted child?

A: Some families elect to use "birth mother" and "birth father," terms which are probably most popular within adoptive groups today. "Biological parents" or "bioparents" are the words chosen by many, words which are scientific in tone. Some use the rather cumbersome but descriptive phrase "man and woman who gave birth."

The term "natural mother" is still commonly used today. The media are fond of it, and it was used frequently to describe the surrogate mother in a recent court case. While the intent evidently is to interchange "natural" with "biological," there is a tremendous difference in the connotations of the two words. "If she is the 'natural mother,'" says one adoptive mother, "what am I? The 'unnatural mother'? Please just say 'biological.'"

It can be noted that these terms have in common the avoidance of the phrase "real parent." The "real parent" is the one who cares for and nurtures the child. If a child suggests, upon learning about his friend's adoption, "Then Mrs. Jones is not Billy's real mother," he can be corrected with the assertion, "Oh, Mrs. Jones is Billy's real mother. Another woman gave birth

14

to Billy, but the woman who raises a child is his real mother."

We prefer "biological mother" and "biological father."

Once adoptive parents have made their notes, they can distribute copies to those persons who will be likely to have considerable contact with their child. Friends, relatives, neighbors, car-pool moms (many conversations regarding adoption seem to take place in cars!), teachers, club leaders, physicians, even grandparents are often at a loss as to which words to choose and would benefit from a personalized copy of this manual. The local school, day-care center, library, church office, your adoption agency or private placement attorney, a friend who is a counselor may find it useful to have a copy which is not annotated. You may decide to list all the names of moms in your child's play group in one book, asking them to pass it on to the next person after reading.*

A final suggestion to non-adoptive parents and other caring adults is that they approach this subject with a tone of casualness. Adoption is, after all, merely one of the ways of having a baby enter the family. A "matter-of-fact" approach on the part of all adults will help the biological child accept his friend's adoption in like manner. It is not a secretive issue or a scary issue, nor is it one of which to boast. It is simply factual.

Remember, the reaction of an adopted child's friends toward his adoption is important to his self-image and his self-esteem. The concern evidenced by a non-adoptive parent's or other adult's willingness to read this guide and to deliver with care his explanation and responses regarding adoption is deeply appreciated.

*Order forms are included at the end of this book for your convenience.

Chapter Three ~

Questions and Answers

Question One ~

Q: What is adoption? What does "being adopted" mean?

A: Adoption is one way of building a family. There are many ways of having a baby enter a family, but two methods are very common. The most usual way is for a woman to go to the hospital and have a baby born from her uterus. Another common way is for a husband and wife to go to an adoption agency where they are presented with a baby who needs a home.

At that time, legal papers which are required by law are signed. The child is given the name of his adoptive parents, and legally it is the same as if he were born to them. The baby becomes their child and is a part of their family forever.

The United Nations Draft Declaration relating to the protection and welfare of children states this formally but clearly: "The primary purpose of adoption is to provide a permanent family for a child who cannot be cared for by his/her biological family."

Question Two ~

Q: Why didn't the adoptive parents just "have" a child instead of adopting one?

A: Generally, the reason is medical. Sometimes bearing a child would be a risk to the woman's health. Sometimes one parent has a genetic problem (severe corneal condition, for example) that the couple chooses not to pass on to offspring, and therefore decides to adopt. Often the couple cannot, for any of a variety of reasons, conceive a child, and adoption is an alternate way of being able to have a family.

This type of information is often private in nature. It certainly should not be shared with a young child, and perhaps should be shared only with the approval of the couple involved.

Suffice it to say, especially to a young child, "The Joneses wanted a family for a long time. When it didn't happen, they decided to adopt a child, and were they excited when the baby arrived!"

Question Three ~

Q: When did the woman who gave birth decide to allow the child to be adopted?

A: Usually long before the child was born. Especially if she were a very young girl, she probably discussed with her own parents what she should do, and together they decided on a course of action.

Of course, only the birth mother (and the birth father if he is available) can actually sign the legal papers that release the child for adoption. But often she has had the assistance of parents, counselors, clergy or other adult friends in making this difficult decision.

In the case of agency adoptions, trained pregnancy counselors are usually available to outline all feasible alternatives to the biological parents prior to their deciding whether or not to transfer their parental rights.

Question Four ~

Q: Why was the child allowed to be adopted?

A: Most commonly, the man and woman who gave birth were very young and felt unable to be responsible parents or to cope with parenthood at that particular time. A straightforward answer such as this is preferable to "They gave him up because they loved him so much." This could lead a child to mistrust love, to wonder if he'll be given away if he is loved. The biological parents are valued for the gift they gave the child, the gift of life. They simply were unable to raise a child, any child, at that time.

Sometimes the man and woman who gave birth have died. Sometimes, in war-torn countries, children have been separated from parents and have then been adopted by another family. At times parents in such a country have seen that there is no hope for their child to grow up safely there, and so they have sought an adoptive situation in another place. Often, the man and woman who gave birth in another country and decided to allow the child to be adopted and come to this country were very young and could not raise a child at that time.

An adopted child may or may not be aware of the particulars of his situation. Adoptive parents are careful to be as straightforward as possible about this subject in order to avoid inducing fantasies in their children. Adopted children tend to blame themselves—thinking they were bad or weren't good enough in some way—and thus were not acceptable to the biological parents. Therefore the actual reason, devoid of embellishment, is in order. This is a sensitive question, highly personal in nature, and probably should be pursued only if volunteered by the adopted child.

Question Five ~

Q: Where was your adopted child born?

A: In a hospital, with doctors and nurses present, just as is usually the case with a biological child.

When an adopted child asks this question, it's probably reassurance he wants, reassurance that he isn't so different after all, even though the family he belongs to is not the one into which he was born.

In many cases, the actual place of birth is not known to the adoptive parents (although this varies with private adoptions and some agency adoptions). But an answer of "I don't know" to this query could make an adopted child feel more different than he need feel. He is like every other child in that he was born in a hospital from the uterus of a woman, and doctors and nurses were present. (The occasional taxicab syndrome need not be discussed here!)

If in fact the name of the hospital is not known, the child can certainly be told "We don't know which hospital." But we can help to alleviate the adopted child's feeling of not knowing "who he is" by cushioning the fact that we don't know the exact point of his origin with facts that we do know about his birth.

In like manner, a biological child can be helped to see the similarities rather than the differences between himself and his adopted friend.

Question Six ~

Q: Where was your adopted child, physically, before he came to you?

A: The answer to this question varies with the type of adoption and the age of the child. In the case of a very typical agency adoption of an infant, the child is born in a hospital with doctors and nurses in attendance. He will stay in the hospital for the usual number of days, three to seven, depending upon whether there are any physical complications.

Although the practice of using foster homes is changing in favor of more direct and quicker placement, the child involved in an agency adoption will still often be taken to a temporary home where he will be cared for by a "foster mother," a woman (or sometimes a family) who has agreed to care for children prior to the time of their adoption. The foster mother is paid to perform this service, but she is a person who loves babies and is carefully selected by the agency for this task.

The child usually lives in the foster home for two to three weeks, sometimes much longer. The reason that the child is kept in the foster home is to allow time for the man and woman who gave birth to legally sign the papers which will allow the baby to be adopted. They are able during this time period to think rationally and seriously about whether they feel they can handle parenthood at that particular time or if they should sign papers that would allow the child to be adopted. If in fact they sign the papers, the adoptive couple, who has previously been screened and approved by the agency and is now awaiting its child, is told of the little girl or little boy.

The couple meets often as soon as the next day with the caseworker at the agency. They are told about the child and as much about the man and woman who gave birth as has been made available, medical history, physical characteristics, etc.

And then it is time for them to meet the baby, a very emotional moment indeed! If they all like each other (and I have yet to hear of a situation where they didn't), the adoptive couple signs the legal papers that make the child a part of their new family forever.

Question Seven ~

Q: Did your adopted child have a different name before he came to you?

A: Adoptive parents usually do not know the answer to this question.

Any child born in this country is automatically given the last name of the woman who gave birth to him. If an infant or a young child is adopted, the clerk of the court will issue a new birth certificate with the adopted child's new name. The old birth certificate is sealed and deposited into confidential court files.

A struggle emerged in the 1970's to allow adopted persons access to these records once they become adults. However, according to the latest information gathered by The National Committee for Adoption, in all but three states the records presently remain sealed.

Question Eight ~

Q: Why are some adopted children of a different race and some of the same race as their adoptive families?

A: Some adoptive parents think it is better for their particular family if they and the children are of the same race. There are fewer quizzical glances, fewer questions if a black family adopts a black child, if a white family adopts a white child, if an Asian family adopts an Asian child. Some have in their extended family grandparents or aunts and uncles who won't accept as "family" a child of a different race, and who may feel different about such a child or exclude him in some material way such as in a will. (Such a situation is not unheard of, even today, in adoptive families of a single race.)

Some adoptive parents, on the other hand, feel an interracial situation is right for them, that it adds another dimension to adoption, and they welcome exploring a new culture and learning about a heritage new to their family. Robin B. Allen, executive director of The Barker Foundation, a private child placing agency in the District of Columbia and Virginia, further adds: "Some people feel that the love of family members will transcend racial barriers. They acknowledge the difficulties but feel that it is more important for a child to have a permanent family than to be of the same race."

Children adopted into a family of a different race are very visible to the general public, and therefore many children have gotten the idea that all adopted children are of a race different from that of their adoptive families. In addition, some international adoption situations, the airlift of Cambodian children to this country near the end of the Vietnam War, for instance, were highly publicized and therefore contributed to the stereotype.

Moreover, countries that have been open to international adoptions have enhanced this picture. Korea has been open for some time, and adoptive parents across the United States have received Korean children who needed families. The Vietnam conflict years brought numbers of Vietnamese and Cambodian children to this country. So common was this occurrence in many communities that one seven-year-old Caucasian girl was unable to convince her schoolmates that she, too, was adopted by her Caucasian parents!

International adoptions have long been a subject of controversy. Some agencies refuse to arrange such adoptions. Some ethnic groups refuse to support them.

But as Robin Allen so astutely points out, "Interracial adoption causes everyone to evaluate the importance of 'differentness' especially because of the physical difference. It demands that each person consider for himself whether 'family' automatically means 'sameness.' Our society has a need to have children look like their parents. Our society is not as comfortable with difference. In terms of what helps a child with all this, he should be encouraged to think through the *similarities* between people of different races—especially the need of every child for a loving family."

Question Nine ~

Q: Can a single person adopt a child?

A: Yes, adoption by single adults, though far from commonplace, has recently moved from the category of the "unusual." Perhaps because of the growing number of singles in our society today, many of whom have maternal or paternal desires even if they are not married, perhaps because of the diversity in the make-up of families in recent decades, numbers of single women and some single men are adopting children. Older children, who can be in school while the single parent is at work, are most commonly adopted into one-parent families.

Question Ten ~

Q: What is an adoption agency?

A: An adoption agency is a place where there are people who help parents to adopt children and children to adopt parents. Although there are many ways to arrange for the adoption of a child, arrangement through an adoption agency is a common method.

Typically, a couple who wishes to adopt a child will contact an adoption agency to learn if they can submit their names as people who are interested in adoption. Sometimes the agency has had so many such inquiries that they have to tell the callers that they are not presently taking names. This can lead to more searching by the would-be adoptive couple, who may choose another agency, may seek a private adoption situation, or may search for a direct international adoption opportunity.

Often there are "parent support groups" in the area that can be helpful to people who are having difficulty with the adoption process or for some reason have decided to adopt outside an agency. Often single people or couples over the age limit set by agencies who would like to adopt a child can be helped by support groups who will share contacts and knowledge.

If, on the other hand, the couple is lucky enough to be allowed to leave their names with the adoption agency, a packet of papers will eventually arrive by mail. Information is asked about the would-be parents, who realize that the paperwork is no guarantee that they will be allowed to adopt a child. After the required forms have been submitted to the agency, the couple may feel quite encouraged by a home-visit from an agency social worker and by a request from the agency that they have medical examinations and submit the medical reports to the agency.

When all information is collected, the agency uses its own criteria and judgment to determine whether a couple would in fact be desirable parents for a child who needs a home. At this point, the couple is told either that they will eventually receive a child (but the waiting period may be long) or that they will need to look elsewhere for a child.

At the same time a woman, often a young girl, has found herself to be pregnant and feels she cannot manage parenthood at that particular time. She contacts the adoption agency, and a caseworker is assigned to assist through the remainder of the pregnancy and until she has made her final decision as to whether she will allow her child to be adopted. The privacy of the biological parents is honored to the extent that it is their wish, and to the extent that the laws in their particular state demand. But as much information as possible is obtained about the biological parents (medical history, etc.) so that it can be passed on by the agency to the adoptive parents.

The agency will help to arrange medical care for the pregnant woman if need be, or a place to stay outside her neighborhood until delivery of the baby if she chooses.

And so an adoption agency gives assistance to biological parents as well as to would-be adoptive parents. It attempts to take into account the needs and wishes of all people involved, and all the while keeping as its top priority the finding of the best situation for the child.

Question Eleven ~

Q: Did you get to "pick out" your adopted child?

A: No. Adoptive parents do not "pick out" their child. At no point is there a row of babies from which prospective parents make a selection.

If the child is adopted through an agency, and if the child is of the same race as the adoptive parents, effort is put into "matching" the child and an appropriate adoptive family. Sometimes the man and woman who gave birth make specific requests (that the baby be raised in a home that subscribes to a particular religion, for example) and every effort is made to fulfill that request.

Sometimes an effort is made to match physical characteristics of the baby (based on characteristics of the man and woman who gave birth) with the adoptive parents. This of course cannot always be done, and is in fact not thought to be important by some people and agencies.

Often it is a matter of timing: A family has been approved by the agency and is waiting .... A child is born and is waiting ....

Question Twelve ~

Q: Can someone who is no longer a baby be adopted?

A: Yes. There is no age limit on adoption. Even an adult can be adopted. Adoption is a legal process that results in a change of the adopted person's name to that of his new family, and in a new status in terms of inheritance laws.

Question Thirteen ~

Q: How much did you pay for him?

A: Adoptive parents do not pay for a baby. They pay to have work done in order that they can adopt a baby. Fees that are charged an adopting couple are used to support the work of the agency.

Adoption involves the time and efforts of numerous people who give service to biological parents, would-be adoptive parents and babies. Each step of the procedure involves the work of highly trained professionals.

In addition, agencies and private placement attorneys must keep up to date on the laws and regulations concerning adoptions. They must pay rent or upkeep for their facility, and at times need to seek their own legal counsel.

The fee that adoptive parents pay when they receive a baby pays bills incurred by the agency as well as salaries of caseworkers, secretaries, the director, and others. Some states have individually set limits on the amount that an agency can charge for its services, thus keeping the possibility of adoption within the financial reach of most Americans.

In the case of a private adoption, the law in most states requires that the adopting parents pay only for the prenatal care, for the physician's services, and for the hospital bill. This is meant to defray the medical costs incurred by the woman giving birth. These expenses are often not covered by her parent's health insurance, if they have it, as pregnancy of a minor (under age 18) is usually excluded from coverage. In most cases, no other payments, except for attorney fees, are allowed.

Question Fourteen ~

Q: What do you call the man and woman who gave birth to your adopted child?

A: Some families elect to use "birth mother" and "birth father," terms which are probably most popular within adoptive groups today. "Biological parents" or "bioparents" are the words chosen by many, words which are scientific in tone. Some use the rather cumbersome but descriptive phrase "man and woman who gave birth."

The term "natural mother" is still commonly used today. The media are fond of it, and it was used frequently to describe the surrogate mother in a recent court case. While the intent evidently is to interchange "natural" with "biological," there is a tremendous difference in the connotations of the two words. "If she is the 'natural mother,'" says one adoptive mother, "what am I? The 'unnatural mother'? Please just say 'biological.'"

It can be noted that these terms have in common the avoidance of the phrase "real parent." The "real parent" is the one who cares for and nurtures the child. If a child suggests, upon learning about his friend's adoption, "Then Mrs. Jones is not Billy's real mother," he can be corrected with the assertion, "Oh, Mrs. Jones is Billy's real mother. Another woman gave birth to Billy, but the woman who raises a child is his real mother."

Question Fifteen ~

Q: What does an adopted child know about the man and woman who gave birth to him?

A: An adopted child may know absolutely nothing about the man and woman who gave birth to him, or he may actually have met them or know one or both of them well.

If the adoption is done through an agency, efforts have been made to obtain detailed information about both the man and woman who gave birth, although this is not always possible. In a typical agency situation, background information that is passed on to adoptive parents includes medical histories of the biological parents as well as their immediate families, physical characteristics, education, interests and hobbies, religion, employment, and nationality background, but their names are not disclosed.

Sometimes the adoption is not handled by an agency but is arranged by a lawyer. The attorney would supply the legal papers, but a caseworker is often involved even in a private situation, and a family study is usually a legal necessity. As much information as possible is learned about the biological parents, and this information is passed on to the adoptive parents. In such a case, the amount of information known about biological parents varies greatly.

Once a child is adopted, whether through an agency or privately, the records are sealed by state law. State laws vary as to what information from those files is available to adopted children. The amount of information adoptive parents share with their child depends upon how much they know and how much they feel the child is ready to hear.

Question Sixteen ~

Q: Can the man or woman who gave birth ever "take back" the adopted child?

A: No, an adopted child cannot be "taken back." A child's adoptive family is his "forever family."

It is possible that the man or woman who gave birth will choose to search for and perhaps locate the child, but the adoption decree is binding. The biological parents no longer retain any legal rights to the child once they allow him to be adopted.

Until recently, laws regarding adoption, although they vary from state to state, were almost uniformly "closed" in that they protected the privacy of the biological parents, adoptive parents, and the adopted child. Once the adoption was finalized, the original birth certificate was "sealed" by the court and would not be revealed even for the most dire medical emergency.

In recent years, however, adoption laws in virtually every state are being reexamined and acted upon. Various approaches are being considered. The "open record" approach is favored in a very few states. A voluntary registry has been instituted in some, encouraging adopted persons, adoptive parents, as well as birth parents, to register and hope for a "match."

The intermediary approach is one in which a trained professional will engage in outreach for the person sought if the reason is deemed appropriate. Any one of the individuals involved, including adult siblings, could initiate the request.

In addition, private "search" groups are in the business (some using legal means and some not) of finding a person being sought. Reasons for such an outreach vary from medical emergencies to a felt need to search for biological roots or offspring.

Whatever the cause or whomever the initiator, the legalities are the same. The adopted child remains a part of his adoptive family forever.

Question Seventeen ~

Q: Will your child ever search for the man and woman who gave birth to him?

A: Maybe, but this question can only be answered with the inconclusive statistic that more adopted girls are interested in searching for biological parents than are adopted boys. In addition, more adopted persons are interested in initiating such a search if they have been told very little about the biological parents.

Sometimes adopted persons decide to let the unknown be. Some express indifference to their biological roots. Some, on the other hand, choose to search, not because they are unhappy, but simply to know. Many express the desire to look into eyes and faces that mirror their own facial features. One wanted to be sure that her birth mother "had only two eyes, one nose, and one mouth like everybody else."

The overwhelming number of adopted persons who search for their biological roots do so for the above reasons, and definitely not to replace their adoptive families. Some, in fact, are curious but are hesitant to initiate a search because they think their adoptive parents might feel threatened.

Some adoptive parents encourage a search and offer assistance to their children when they reach a certain age. Some feel less comfortable, sometimes out of concern for the privacy of the biological parents, sometimes because they feel they might in some way lose the child who means the world to them.

Interestingly, "adoption fantasies" are common to most children, biological or adopted. "Certainly I must *really* have come from a perfect family and my mother was a princess who would never discipline me" is the usual tone.

The adopted child often has this or a similar fantasy. He also has a reality to face: He doesn't know his biological origin. How he chooses to deal with this fact has to be a strictly personal decision. What is right for him may or may not be right for another adopted person.

Should an adopted child bring this subject up in conversation with you, and only if he brings it up, it would be helpful if you would simply allow him to talk, ask him appropriate questions, and let him talk some more. You are important to him if he has chosen to share his thoughts on this subject with you. But he's probably not asking for advice; he simply needs an ear.

Question Eighteen ~

Q: What if the parents of an adopted child get a divorce?

A: In case of divorce or legal separation, an adopted child is treated by the courts exactly the same as if he were a birth child of that couple. A separation or divorce would have no effect whatsoever upon the adoption itself. Even if the marriage were annulled, the adoption decree would be binding. Custody and child support questions would be determined by the judge in the best interests of the child as is the case in any divorce.

Question Nineteen ~

Q: When did you tell your child he was adopted, and when should I tell mine that his friend was adopted?

A: The widely-accepted statement within adoptive circles today is that an adopted child "should never remember a time when he didn't know." The debate is over how much he should know at each stage and when.

Most parents tend to begin by using the word "adopted" casually within their families, perhaps telling the story of "coming home from the adoption agency after we had adopted you, what you wore, the cute blanket in your crib, how happy mommy and daddy were"—much as one does with a birth child. So the concept is there very early but most families today wait for the questions before explaining more. The rather "even years," developmentally speaking, of seven through ten are thought to be an ideal time for the adopted child to learn more, although of course questions need to be handled as they arise.

Probably the adopted child will mention the fact of his adoption to his friends. The friends will ask questions first of him and then of their own parents. Waiting for this opener may be the best way to proceed. Any manner of the "There is something I need to tell you about Johnny . . ." approach would add undue emphasis to the subject.

Question Twenty ~

Q: If my biological child asks about your child's adoption, should I go into depth about the hows and whys?

A: In such a situation, the age of the child doing the questioning needs to be taken into account. Consider for a moment the parallel biological facts that you have at your disposal regarding the planning of your birth baby: of his conception, of his gestation, of his birth. Certain of those facts you deem appropriate to share with your four-year-old or your six-year-old. Certain of them you don't.

Translate this data, if you would, into the adoption process. Are the details of the adoptive parents' inability to conceive a child, for example, appropriately told to your four-year-old, your six-year-old.

An axiom heard at meetings of adoptive parents but valid in all parenting experiences is: Tell the truth from the beginning. You never want to have to undo what you have said.

On the other hand, the amount of information given

to a young child is critical, and certainly the privacy of the adoptive couple and the adopted child deserves foremost consideration here. Perhaps the questions that seem too personal could be truthfully answered, "I guess I don't know. I am certainly glad, though, that Johnny is a part of the Jones family."

Question Twenty-One ~

Q: How does the adopted child feel toward his adoptive family?

A: Sometimes fine. Sometimes angry. Sometimes cheated. Sometimes lucky. Sometimes he wonders if he's loved. Sometimes he knows how much he's loved.

One adopted girl says she feels like she came from another planet. One adopted boy says he's not really curious about his biological parents—he's happy with this family, and he adds, "The rest of you haven't met all your genetic ancestors either."

Some say, "I'm adopted. That's the breaks," and go on with their lives with their adoptive families. Others feel resentment toward their adoptive families, almost blaming them for being there, perhaps unwittingly and incorrectly feeling that the birth parents might not have allowed the adoption had this family not been standing there with open arms.

Some are reassured by the fact that these are their "parents for keeps." The closeness between them is based on their lives together and their love for each other—not on the accident of birth.

Many feel all of the above emotions—at different times and in response to different situations.

In short, the feelings of an adopted child toward his adoptive family are about as mixed and changeable and changing as are the feelings of a biological child toward his family.

Question Twenty-Two ~

Q: What should I say if your adopted adolescent child sounds negative about his adoption or adoptive family?

A: As he struggles to find that balance between independence from and dependence on his parents, the adopted adolescent may well "hang the blame" for all his woes upon his adoption. Remember that a birth child will similarly find something or other to blame. The adopted child simply has a very convenient whipping post. Assuring him that family life can indeed be a challenge would be helpful.

Talking about his fears and angers is the healthiest thing he can do and saying it doesn't make it worse; it works as a catharsis. An adopted child needs empathy and a listening ear as much as does a birth child. Certainly you don't want to encourage him to wallow in self-pity, but don't be afraid of letting him express himself. If you get the uncomfortable feeling of being out of your depth, perhaps you can encourage the young person to talk to his parents and school counselor about his feelings.

Question Twenty-Three ~

Q: What if my biological child asks a question not covered in this guide and for which I have no answer?

A: Adoptive parents are also put in this position by their children at times. Often an involved question is asked just as guests are arriving for a dinner party. Or the question is one that Mom really would like to discuss with Dad before answering. In such situations, a simple "I can't answer you right now, but I will tell you tomorrow" will give parents time to think or possibly to confer with the adoptive parents or to consult another resource.

Of course, be sure to answer tomorrow.

Question Twenty-Four ~

Q: Are there sensitive expressions to avoid when talking to an adopted child?

A: Parents of birth children can probably get away with the teasing, "He's in the tantrum stage. We're ready to send him back where he came from." A statement such as this must never be made, no matter how obvious the joke, regarding an adopted child. The fear of just such a scenario often lurks not far from the surface of an adopted child's consciousness.

Some adoptive parents are comfortable with the "chosen baby" phrase. Some are concerned that any emphasis on the "chosen" aspect could raise the fear in an adopted child that, if chosen, he could just as easily be "un-chosen."

Question Twenty-Five ~

Q: Should I refer to your adopted child as being somehow "special"? Is it more wonderful to be adopted, or to be a birth baby?

A: These are simply two different ways of having a family. Neither is preferable. The important thing is that birth parents and adoptive parents alike want to have a family, and they are delighted when the baby arrives, by whatever method.

Question Twenty-Six ~

Q: How do you refer to a sibling who was not adopted?

A: Somewhere between 11 and 14 percent of the families who adopt a child will later conceive and give birth. In addition, families with one biological child often are unable to have a second, and decide to adopt. Numerous families, therefore, are composed of both "birth" children and adopted children.

The term "birth" child, popular now among many adoptive groups, is used in an attempt to find a parallel term for the process of adoption. "Biological" child is a term preferred by many, and describes the distinction rather scientifically. The term "natural" child is preferred by some, but to others suggests the uncomfortable opposite of "unnatural."

Question Twenty-Seven ~

Q: What's in the heart of adoptive parents? Is there a different quality to the love they feel toward an adopted child as compared with a birth child?

A: Someone who is not an adoptive parent might assume there is a difference in the feelings, but the answer is a resounding NO. As Richard Cohen observed in "A Child of One's Own" for the Washington Post Magazine, "The people I know who have adopted children love them no less because they are not 'their own.' In some ways, maybe, they love them more. Whatever the case, they love them. God, how they love those kids."

This is not to say there is no awareness that the child is adopted. That would amount to a denial of reality, the reality that a set of birth parents exists somewhere, that the child's biological roots are elsewhere. But that does not change the quality of the love adoptive parents feel for their child.

Consider for a moment this often-told story. An adoptive mother, Mary, and her friend Peggy, a non-adoptive mother, read a newspaper article. Two ten-

61

year-old children, it was recently determined, had been accidentally switched as infants in the hospital and had grown up in the 'wrong' families.

Peggy's immediate response was, "But of course they should have their own children back."

Mary gently replied, "Peggy, your daughter is ten. If she were one of those children, would you want to switch now?"

An adoptive family, like a biological family, wants a child, and when that child comes to them, by whatever method, they have the same kind of love in their hearts for him. And the bond between a parent and a child is built on love and obligation and trust—not on blood.

There may be an additional dimension to the feelings in the hearts of adoptive parents. Both families, the biological and adoptive, are thankful for their child. The adoptive family is thankful for the child, but there's more than that. They are also thankful *to* someone, someone who gave them an incredible gift.

Question Twenty-Eight ~

Q: Is an adopted baby your "real" sister, your "real" child?

A: Absolutely. An adopted child is as much a "real" member of the family as is a birth child. Blood is only one factor in relationship. A husband and wife, after all, are not blood relatives, and yet they certainly are members of the family. Adopted means belonging.

However, this question answered thoughtlessly led to this actual conversation. Billy, a five-year-old biological child of the Smiths, announced to his parents one morning, "Suzie is not my sister." When questioned about his statement, Billy elaborated on the conversation he had had on the previous day with his five-year-old friend, Sam. "Sam said Suzie is not my real sister because she is adopted."

"That's not true," his parents gently insisted. "You are our son. Suzie is our daughter. You know that Suzie was adopted and that you were born from Mommy's uterus in the hospital, but those are just two different ways of coming into a family. You are Suzie's brother, and Suzie is your sister.

There are many things that Mom and Dad don't know for sure, Billy, and we will always tell you if we aren't sure of something. You asked last week how the planets were made, and we told you what some scientists think happened, but that we don't know for sure. But this is something we do know for sure. Your friend Sam is wrong about what he said. Suzie absolutely is your sister."

Question Twenty-Nine ~

Q: Can an adopted child marry a sibling?

A: When a child asks this question, it is often out of a biological concern. He may have learned that relatives are not allowed to marry because they are likely to produce abnormal offspring and he may wonder if that would be true of adopted siblings if they were not related by blood.

While adopted siblings would produce healthy children, state laws prohibit such marriages since this would undermine the social purpose which adoption serves. The prohibition can be stated or implied.

Historically, a few legal cases involve young people who had been adopted in their older teens when their parents married and adopted each other's children. The young people had not been raised together but were now technically siblings. They took their desire to marry to the courts. One state allowed the marriage; another faced with a similar situation did not.

Complicated exceptions aside, the answer is that siblings are not allowed to marry, and adopted siblings are siblings.

Question Thirty ~

Q: What are some "nevers" to remember when we are in the presence of adopted children.

A: ~ Never, during introductions, say, "This is the Blacks' adopted son, Billy." Would you ever say, "This is Mary, the Browns' birth baby"?

~ Never ask an adoptive parent in the presence of the children, "Which is your adopted child?"

~ Never say to newly adoptive parents, "Now you'll have one of your own." First of all, this baby is "Their Own." Secondly, it is difficult to describe the pain a couple has gone through prior to receiving this child into their arms and hearts. True, couples sometimes do conceive after adopting. But that does not happen as often as it might seem from the stories that abound. At any rate, be pleased for the new family, but spare them the teasing. They may still be raw and hurting.

~ Never stop an interracial adoptive family on the street to share with them your own stories of friends and relatives who have similarly adopted international children. Your intentions are surely supportive, but one such family says that this occurrence, which happens quite often, makes them feel like a side-show.

~ Never ask an adopted child, or her adoptive parents, about her origin. This information is strictly for the family. On the other hand, should the adopted child choose to talk to you about it, a listening ear would be most helpful.

~ Never make "more of a fuss" over an adopted child in a family than you do over a biological sibling. Actually it's preferable to overlook the distinction and treat both children, the adopted and the biological, just like everyone else's kids.

Question Thirty-One ~

Q: Is it all right to say your adopted child is "lucky to have found such a good home"?

A: We're all lucky. We're lucky to be a family. But it's not an idea we would like presented to an adopted child anymore than to a birth child. Any feeling of being beholden or in debt to an adoptive family could cause unnecessary resentment in the child.

There was a time when children who needed homes were in abundance and it was common for a family to consider doing a service for society or to perform what they felt was a religious service by raising such a child. An adopted child was considered "lucky."

Today the picture has changed. For a number of reasons, fewer children are born into situations in which birth parents or the birth mother decides not to parent the child. As a result, babies are sought, sometimes desperately, by childless couples. Indeed, it is the adoptive family that feels "lucky to have found a child."

Question Thirty-Two ~

And finally,

Q: Do you "love her like your own"?

A: She is.

Chapter Four ~

Why the Secrecy?

Chapter Four ~ As I was asking businesses for financial support for an adoption agency, I encountered one day a middle-aged businessman who listened carefully to my presentation and then leaned forward in a rather conspiratorial way. He glanced over one shoulder and then the other to be certain no one was within hearing distance. He cleared his throat and in a low voice said, "I would like to help your agency. I am an adopted person, too."

I received the money as I had hoped, but my memory of the encounter continued to bother me. Why had this very successful and charming man felt the need to be secretive?

I know also an elderly gentleman who had been adopted as an infant, but supposedly doesn't know of his adoption to this day.

Why? Why, in the past, was adoption often regarded as a fact to be kept secret?

The amount of backslapping that Dad receives when cigars are handed out hints of macho-ism. Protection for an infertile couple from a society which equated manhood with the ability to impregnate seems to have encouraged secrecy regarding adoption. Fear played a part in perpetuating secrecy. Fear of hereditary ramifications, fear of the return of a biological parent, fear of scandal due to incest or sexual indiscretion.

Was the basis partially religious? Did the attitude originate with our Puritan ancestors who frowned upon illicit sexual unions. Research shows that the attitude, which encouraged people to hide the fact of adoption from children born in those circumstances, predates the Puritans.

Adoption, though not always formal or legalized, is common to all societies and has been throughout recorded history. Sometimes for reasons of maintaining family lines with heirs, for reasons of inheritance, for extending the family for mutual protection, for passing on a craft or trade within the family—these and other situations encouraged societies, from the most primitive to the most advanced, to view adoption as a logical and compassionate act.

The ancient Greeks, Romans, Egyptians, and Babylonians practiced adoption. The Babylonian Code of Hammurabi of the 18th century B.C. discusses adoption at length. Among these peoples, adoption served as a way of providing a male heir to a childless couple for reasons of inheritance, for the performing of certain religious rites, and (have we discovered the genesis of baby-kissing by our politicians?) in Rome, a person was considered a better candidate for public office if he had more children than his opponent!

Yet with such a history, adoption is still thought of by many people as an unusual step. In a society where bloodlines play almost no role in the understanding of a person's place in society or of his identity, adoptions are taken for granted. In Polynesia, for example, the origins of every family are traced to mythical founders, and a person's biological ancestry is unimportant.

Why, then, if adoption has been accepted by most societies down through the years, did Americans, usually such a practical people and a people quite unconcerned with bloodlines, develop feelings that would encourage adoptive parents in years past to deny, sometimes even to themselves, that a child was adopted?

The basis of this attitude appears to have grown out of British common law, upon which our laws are based, and which did not recognize adoption. Our actual adoption laws are based upon Roman law, but our legal system as a whole is derived from the British common law system.

Blood ties were stressed by English nobility more so than by any other group in history. Property and titles passed from father to son, or to other male relatives if necessary. In the absence of male relatives, titles and property fell out of use. Informal adoptions were common, but informally adopted persons were left in legal limbo, and Heathcliffs abound in English literature.

And so a child adopted in the United States must face that legacy, the historical feelings on the part of society that adoption is somehow extraordinary or especially noteworthy.

A reaction to this attitude was evident when, in the 1960's, American adoptive parents were encouraged to remind their child daily that "You are our beautiful adopted daughter," and the yearly "coming home" celebration was practiced with the gusto of a birthday party.

After all but disappearing in Europe during the Middle Ages in favor of indenture, legal adoption was introduced again in the mid-19th century. Concern at that juncture was protection of the rights of adoptive parents who feared birth parents might attempt to reclaim the child, especially if there were some financial advantage.

The first U.S. laws regarding adoption were passed in Texas and Vermont in 1850. These laws simply made "public record of private agreements of adoption." In 1851, Massachusetts followed with the first law to provide for judicial supervision of adoption, calling for a judgment to be made of the parents' ability to provide for the child.

Adoption law in the United States slowly evolved to protect not only the rights of adoptive parents, but the rights of the adopted child as well, and the privacy of the biological parents. And England did legalize adoption in 1926.

But the legal rights of adopted children have been hard-won. Issues of inheritance are the usual troublesome area. Of such importance is inheritance that today in "countries such as France, Greece, Spain, and most of Latin America, adoption is prohibited when it would change inheritance rights of biological children." Even in the United States, adoptive parents are warned to be sure their wills and the wills of grandparents are carefully screened to be certain the adopted child is not inadvertently excluded by such terms as "issue of your body."

After World War II, numerous adoption agencies came into being and standardization of procedures appeared. In the 1950's, half the non-relative adoptions in the U.S. were agency placements. The baby boom led to a doubling of the number of adoptions from 1952 to 1970, and the trend toward agency adoptions continued. In 1971, only 20 percent of the adoptions in the U.S. were independent or non-agency placements.

Suddenly the 1970's happened. The baby boom came to an end. Presently 15 to 20 couples wait for every healthy white infant. In 1970, single mothers allowed 80 to 90 percent of their babies to be adopted. By 1975, 80 to 90 percent of the single mothers decided to parent their babies. At the same time, a push began for the opening of sealed records. England passed laws allowing the 18-year-old adopted person to sit down with a special counselor and learn the facts of his past.

Presently, when children in need of homes are desperately sought by the ever-increasing number of infertile couples, when legal battles rage between surrogate and would-be adoptive mothers, perhaps the attitude pendulum can swing once more and land in the middle—a middle where adoption is neither denied nor newsworthy, but where it is accepted for what it is: one of the methods of having a child enter a family.

Chapter Five ~

Consciousness Raising

Chapter Five ~ "Have you finished your Christmas shopping?" I overheard one grocery clerk ask another. "No," was the icy reply. "I haven't done my Christmas shopping because I'm not Christian."

"Oops. Sorry," said the offending clerk. "Have you finished your holiday shopping yet?"

The vignette illustrates what happens when majorities act like majorities, and how changes, even such small ones of language, can be important. Remember when black people were colored and a female secretary was a girl.

Such changes in phraseology, minimal as they seem, are very difficult ones to accomplish . . . but possible. Similarly, it will take conscious effort on the part of people in non-adoptive situations to use thoughtful words when referring to adoption.

There exists in our country a bias about adoption, a bias as divisive as religious or racial or sexual bias. At the worst level is the open bigotry. An occasional stage play will include a crude adoption joke, and children's cartoons depicting Mama and Papa Mouse who wanted to adopt a baby and ended up with a baby cat, dropped by mistake by the stork, are commonplace. Thoughtless, pointless words and ideas such as these are, like racial jokes, in very poor taste, and the world would be a better place without them.

On another level is the bias displayed by those who at the conscious level are supportive of adoption, but whose actions betray their prejudice.

An interesting phenomenon presented itself during the 1984 Winter Olympics. Several of the American gold medalists, as it turned out, had been adopted as children. It was as if a new species had been discovered. Reporters were relentless in pursuing the adoptive mothers and fathers about this issue. To their credit, the adoptive parents answered patiently and with more class than I would have displayed, and the adoption details of skaters and skiers were, if not headlined, at least front-page news. No similar birth questions were raised about biological offspring who were winning gold medals.

During my first career as a teacher, I was party to "staffings," weekly sessions conducted by the principal during which teachers discussed problems displayed by various students with the objective of determining how best to help each child. Certainly no overt bias exists in school systems, but in truth I must report that on many occasions in two different states teachers passed around an all-knowing "Ohhh," complete with nod and raised eyebrows, upon learning that a child with some sort of difficulty was an adopted child. Never mind that scores of other children with identical learning problems were discussed each year. The fact of a child's adoption seemed to carry great significance, and I, not knowing that I some day would be an adoptive parent, sat there wondering why, but not having the seniority, or perhaps the courage, to challenge those knowing nods.

The act of doing research for this guide made me aware of another indignity regarding adoption to add to this "Believe It Or Not" chapter. I needed to know the general category of my book in order to apply for a copyright with the Library of Congress. The librarian responded that the 300 books were "Sociology" books. The 362.73 books were—well, they were always being changed; let's look at the most current listing. We found that, in order to find a book about adoption, one must presently go to a section of the public library labeled "Social Pathology and Services." Making an adopted person, an adoptive parent, or the general public sort through "Pathology" in order to reach "Social Services" seems archaic.

As Sheila Macmanus says so elegantly in *The Adoption Book,* "It is very important that we put ideas and words like 'abandon a child' or 'give a child up (for adoption)' behind us as a civilization. It is time we stopped asking, 'Which is your real child?' It is time we celebrate the true meanings of parenthood, brotherhood, sisterhood and family by toasting our children with caring words, laws, and attitudes."

I always told my junior high school language arts students that I was teaching them correct grammar so that they could *use* it as they themselves spoke—*not* so that they could criticize others who might use poor grammar. Proper language should be a tool, not a weapon. Likewise, these adoption issues and terms are included here in this same spirit, simply in the cause of awareness and as an aid to us all as we begin to use more constructive speech regarding adoption.

I do not mean to castigate anyone who might have for years been using some of the less desirable terms. We all have. We spoke the words our society handed to us. However, once these words and issues are brought to our attention, we can begin to change our habits of speech, difficult as that admittedly might be.

Another truth complicates the issue of terminology:

Adoptive parents do not always agree among themselves, nor do professionals, as to which terms are preferable. The same can be said of nearly any movement which faces an obsolete vocabulary.

And so these words and ideas are not absolute but are included here to show how the connotations affect some people. They can be a guide to caring and constructive speech, speech which takes into account the feelings of the adoption triad: the biological parents, the adoptive parents, and, of foremost importance, the adopted child.

Since you, the reader, interact with an adopted child, you will have an impact on his life. Even the common uncomfortableness shown by an unprepared adult when asked a question about adoption sends a message. We adoptive parents are truly appreciative of your willingness to familiarize yourself with these issues, to read this book, and to consider the impact of your words and your children's words on our adopted sons and daughters.

There is a special parenting skill required of adoptive parents, and you now share that skill with us. The key, of course, is to imagine the impact of a response from three points of view—the adopted child's, the adoptive parents', and the birth parents'—and to treat all three with respect and valuing. It is not hyperbole to say you are making the lives of adoptive parents easier and the lives of adopted children happier.

Acknowledgments

What a joy it is to work with an editor who can draw upon such a wide range of publishing skills. Friend as much as consultant, Jan Nagel Clarkson has buoyed, calmed, urged, explained, explored, exulted . . . and has been right every time.

For their encouragement, enlightenment, and excitement, I thank:

Sara Akerlund
Robin Allen
Betsy Ambach
Rita Arendal
Barbara Baker
Vern and Hannah Bengtson
Adaline Bjorkman
Vivian Boul
Eleanor Chatfield-Taylor
Jack Corrigan
Carol Craft
Colleen Friedman
Jan Gonder
Cathy Hofgren

Tim and Nancy Johnson
Joan Krinsly
Robin Leech
Marcia McDermott
Sandy and Bonnie Mohlman
Lynne Myers
Al and Kathy Olson
Deirdre Radanovic
Patti Ravenscroft
Martha Ann Richardson
Peggy Ruchti
Elise Smith
Debbie Wood

Paulist Press has generously given permission to quote from *The Adoption Book* by Sheila Macmanus, copyright ©1984 by Sheila Macmanus.

Enclosed is my check or money order for ___ copies of *When Friends Ask About Adoption* at $6.00 ($4.95 + tax and postage).

Please send to:

Name _____
Address _____
City _____
State _____ Zip _____

Ship to: (if different from sold to)

Name _____
Address _____
City _____
State _____ Zip _____

Please mail order form to:
Swan Publications
P.O. Box 15293
Chevy Chase, MD 20815
(202) 244-9092